Technology through the Ages

MEDICINE

THROUGH THE AGES

From Acupuncture to Antibiotics

MICHAEL WOODS AND MARY B. WOODS

T0054319

TWENTY-FIRST CENTURY BOOKS™ / MINNEAPOLIS

For Alexander, Caden, Sophie, Violet, Clara, Maeve, and Orion

Twenty-First Century Books™
An imprint of Lerner Publishing Group, Inc.
241 First Avenue North
Minneapolis, MN 55401 USA

For reading levels and more information, look up this title at www.lernerbooks.com.

Main body text set in Bembo Std Regular.
Typeface provided by Monotype Typography.

Library of Congress Cataloging-in-Publication Data

Names: Woods, Michael, 1946– author. I Woods, Mary B. (Mary Boyle), 1946– author.
Title: Medicine through the ages : from acupuncture to antibiotics / Michael Woods and Mary B. Woods.
Description: Minneapolis : Twenty-First Century Books , [2024] I Series: Technology through the ages I Includes bibliographical references and index. I Audience: Ages 11–18 I Audience: Grades 7–9 I Summary: "Ancient civilizations developed advanced medical techniques and devices that helped to improve and extend people's lives. Uncover the innovation and ingenuity of ancient medical technology and learn how it laid the groundwork for modern medicine"— Provided by publisher.
Identifiers: LCCN 2023005317 (print) I LCCN 2023005318 (ebook) I ISBN 9798765610039 (library binding) I ISBN 9798765619490 (epub)
Subjects: LCSH: Medicine, Ancient—Juvenile literature. I Medical innovations—History—Juvenile literature. I Drugs—History—Juvenile literature. I BISAC: YOUNG ADULT NONFICTION / Health & Daily Living / Diseases, Illnesses & Injuries
Classification: LCC R135 .W735 2024 (print) I LCC R135 (ebook) I DDC 610.938—dc23/eng/20230504

LC record available at https://lccn.loc.gov/2023005317
LC ebook record available at https://lccn.loc.gov/2023005318

Manufactured in the United States of America
1 – CG – 12/15/23

CONTENTS

INTRODUCTION

What do you think of when you hear the word *technology*? You might think of modern research laboratories filled with computers, microscopes, and other scientific tools. But technology doesn't refer to just brand–new machines and discoveries. Technology is as old as humankind.

Technology is the use of knowledge and inventions to make human life better. The word *technology* comes from Greek. *Tekhne* means "art" or "craft." Adding the suffix *-logia* meant the study of arts and crafts. In modern times, the word usually refers to a craft, technique, or tool.

People use technology to farm crops, construct buildings, and get from place to place. This book looks at another important kind of technology: medicine.

A Matter of Life and Death

Ancient peoples were very familiar with sickness and death. In some ancient cultures, one out of every three babies died

This sculpture from Greece shows an early physician treating injured and sick individuals. Sculptures and carvings like this one can shed light on some of the world's oldest medical practices.

before the age of one. Sometimes diseases spread through ancient cities and killed large numbers of people. In 542 CE, plague killed about half the population of Constantinople (modern-day Istanbul, Turkey). Ancient people saw death up close. Many people died at home. Their family members prepared their bodies for burial or cremation. Although illness and death were familiar to them, ancient people were just as eager as modern people to live long, healthy lives. When people got sick or injured, they sought someone to make them well. All ancient societies had healers or physicians. Some ancient societies even had hospitals and medical schools.

Archaeologists can learn a lot about ancient health and medicine by studying human remains. This archaeologist examines human bones from an ancient graveyard in Batroun, Lebanon.

Learning from the Past

Archaeologists study the remains of past cultures. To learn about ancient health and medicine, these scientists must piece together many clues. Some clues come from ancient human bones. Archaeologists can study them to learn how tall ancient people were, whether they had bone disease, or how old they were when they died.

Often ancient people left clear clues about their health and medicine. Some ancient doctors wrote books about illness and medicine. Ancient paintings, drawings, and sculptures often show doctors or other healers at work. Archaeologists have found many ancient medical tools, such as surgeons' scalpels.

A Lot with a Little

Ancient doctors did not have X–ray machines or microscopes. They did not have drugstores full of medicines. But they had just as much curiosity and creativity as modern doctors and scientists. Even without these advanced tools to help them, ancient healers accomplished great things.

CHAPTER ONE
Medical Basics

The first *Homo sapiens*, or modern humans, lived about 300,000 years ago. They lived in small groups. They got their food by hunting game, fishing, and gathering wild plants. When the food in one area was depleted, the group moved to a new place. Hunter-gatherers made tools from stone, wood, animal bones, plant fibers, and clay.

First Aid

Like all people, early hunter-gatherers got injured and got sick. When studying ancient human skeletons, archaeologists often see signs of broken bones, tooth decay, gum disease, and arthritis.

Some medical treatments probably came to ancient people naturally. When you feel pain, instinct tells you to rub the spot that hurts. When you cut your finger, your first reaction might be to grab the finger and squeeze it. The pressure squeezes blood vessels in the finger and helps stop the bleeding. Early humans almost certainly used these kinds of simple treatments.

Archaeologists have found ancient human bones that were broken but then healed. This shows that ancient hunter-gatherers knew how to treat bone fractures. Ancient healers used splints made of wood, animal bone, or other stiff material. The splints kept broken bones straight as they healed.

Early peoples probably discovered many remedies by accident. People ate figs because they were sweet. But people also noticed that figs were natural laxatives, drugs that loosen the bowels. They passed on their knowledge from generation to generation.

Magic Cures

Many ancient cultures believed in gods and spirits. Ancient peoples believed these supernatural beings could cause

These ancient skulls come from what is now London, England. They date from the era of Roman rule there, from the 50s BCE to the 400s CE. The skulls show that these people had diseased teeth.

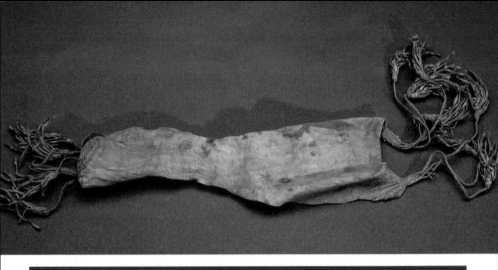

This ancient North American medicine bundle probably contained healing roots, bark, and other plant materials. The bundle might also have held lucky charms, such as animal teeth.

sickness. If someone became ill, people often blamed evil spirits.

To fight evil spirits, ancient people often turned to shamans. They believed that shamans had supernatural healing powers. Shamans treated illness with magic and good luck charms. But they also used effective medicines made from roots, bark, and other parts of plants.

Humans Settle Down

About ten thousand years ago, some people in the Middle East settled down and became farmers. Small farming settlements grew into towns. Towns eventually became cities.

Historians think that early farmers and city dwellers had generally poorer health than hunter-gatherers. In towns and cities, many people lived close together. More people meant more chances for germs to spread. And farmers raised animals such as cows, pigs, goats, chickens, and sheep, which could spread diseases to humans.

A Last Meal

In 2003 workers in Ireland discovered the bodies of two men in peat bogs. Archaeologists determined that they had lived and died between 392 and 175 BCE. The soil in the bogs had preserved the men's bodies and turned them into mummies.

Archaeologists named them Old Croghan Man and Clonycavan Man after the places where they were found. Archaeologists opened Old Croghan Man's stomach. They found that his last meal had consisted of grain and buttermilk. Anthropologists also studied the mummies' heads, bones, and torsos. They determined that Old Croghan Man had died of a stab wound to the chest. Clonycavan Man had been killed by blows to the head and the chest. They were probably made with an axe. No one knows who killed the men or why.

Sometimes the soil in peat bogs preserves dead bodies, making mummies such as Old Croghan Man and Clonycavan Man. This peat bog is in western Ireland.

In ancient towns, people often dumped human waste into the streets. It ran into wells and rivers that supplied drinking water. People who drank that dirty water got sick. Food waste and other garbage also piled up in big trash heaps. The trash attracted flies and other insects that carried disease. Small groups of hunter-gatherers did not live this way. They were regularly on the move, looking for fresh sources of food and clean drinking water.

Some ancient Roman public toilets were connected to sewers to keep waste off the streets. But the sewers emptied into the Tiber River, which many people used for drinking water, bathing, and farming.

Ancient Drug Use

In modern times, thirty-seven US states allow people to use marijuana for medical purposes. And many modern painkilling drugs are opiates. Marijuana comes from the leaves and blossoms of the cannabis plant. Opiates come from opium poppies. Cocaine, a stimulant, comes from coca leaves. These plants have a long history in medicine.

In ancient times, people in many cultures smoked opium to relieve pain, treat illnesses, and bring on sleep. Farmers in southwestern Europe grew opium poppies as early as 6000 BCE. Archaeologists have found ancient statues, jewelry, and other objects depicting opium poppies as well as ancient opium pipes. Traces of coca leaves in northern Peru and Ecuador indicate that people have been chewing coca leaves in South America for thousands of years. Ancient people used cannabis fibers to make rope and textiles. But they also smoked marijuana and drank marijuana tea to treat aching joints, anxiety, and other ailments. The ancient Yamnaya culture of southeastern Europe used cannabis as part of their funeral rites more than five thousand years ago. Writers in ancient Greece, ancient China, and elsewhere wrote about opium and marijuana use. The writers noted that these drugs not only relieved certain ailments but also altered the mind.

This illustration shows an Algonquian shaman. The shaman used medicinal plants as well as magic to cure sick people.

CHAPTER TWO
Ancient Egypt

The first written accounts of ancient medical technology come from Egypt. The ancient Egyptians left detailed medical records. Scribes, or trained writers, wrote down the texts on scrolls of papyrus, a kind of paper made from reeds.

Archaeologists have found Egyptian medical papyruses in ancient tombs. The best known are the Kahun Papyrus, the Edwin Smith Papyrus, and the Ebers Papyrus. The Kahun Papyrus was written around 1900 BCE. It deals with childbirth and gynecology. The Edwin Smith Papyrus, written about 1600 BCE, deals with surgery and the treatment of injuries. The Ebers Papyrus, written around 1550 BCE, is the most famous. It is a medical encyclopedia. It told doctors how to diagnose and treat certain illnesses and how to prepare remedies. It also described how the heart and other human organs function.

The First Known Physician

The first physician historians know by name is the ancient Egyptian Imhotep. Imhotep lived in the 2600s BCE. He was chief

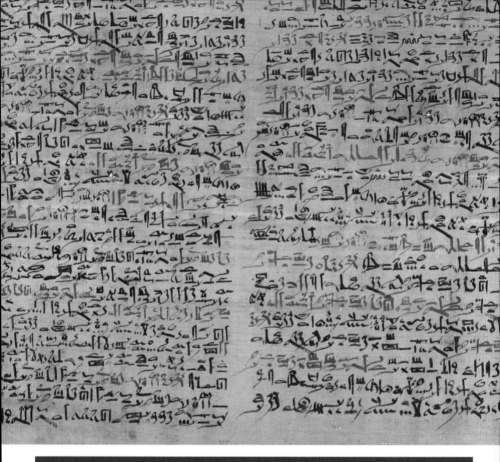

assistant to the Egyptian pharaoh Djoser. Imhotep designed the first pyramid in Egypt, the Pyramid of Djoser at Saqqara. And Imhotep made medicines from plants. He used these remedies to treat people suffering from appendicitis, arthritis, and other ailments. The Egyptians later worshipped Imhotep as a god.

Hesy-Ra is another known ancient physician. He lived in Egypt around 2600 BCE. He worked as "Chief of Physicians and Dentists to the pyramid builders." Egyptian writings say that Hesy-Ra treated decaying teeth and infected gums. He drilled holes into patients' gums to drain pus from infections.

Ahead of the Rest

People in other ancient cultures respected the medical knowledge of Egyptian doctors. Foreign rulers asked Egyptian pharaohs to send doctors to treat them and their families. The ancient Greek poet Homer wrote *The Odyssey* in the late eighth or early seventh century BCE. In this epic poem, Homer described powerful drugs that an Egyptian doctor gave to a Greek queen. He noted that "in medical knowledge the Egyptian leaves the rest of the world behind."

Ancient Egypt had the first medical specialists. These doctors treat specific illnesses or certain parts of the body.

This ancient Egyptian statue shows Imhotep, one of the first known physicians. Imhotep also worked as an architect and as assistant to an Egyptian king in the 2600s BCE.

Originally painted in a tomb, this picture shows an ancient Egyptian doctor treating a patient. The original picture dates from 1292 to 1190 BCE. Later, an artist copied the scene onto papyrus.

The Greek historian Herodotus wrote that "the practice of medicine [the Egyptians] split into separate parts, each doctor being responsible for the treatment of only one disease."

Female doctors may have been common in ancient Egypt. Peseshet, a doctor, lived in Egypt around 2500 BCE. She is the first female physician known by name. Peseshet's title, "Lady Overseer of Lady Physicians," tells us that she was one of many female doctors.

Ready for the Afterlife

The ancient Egyptians believed in an afterlife—or life after death. They wanted to enter the afterlife with their bodies intact. To keep dead bodies from decaying, the ancient Egyptians turned them into mummies. When mummifying bodies, mummy makers removed organs and preserved them in storage jars. They learned a lot about human anatomy. By about 1500 BCE, the ancient Egyptians had perfected mummy-making.

This Egyptian mummy and coffin come from the 1000s or 900s BCE. The mummy is at the British Museum in London, England.

Mrht, Byt, and Ftt

Mrht, *byt*, and *ftt* are the ancient Egyptian words for "grease," "honey," and "lint." Those were the ingredients of a popular Egyptian salve, or ointment. Doctors used the salve to treat cuts, scrapes, and other wounds. This salve, along with these three ingredients, was regularly used in Egyptian medicine.

The grease might have been fat from an ox or another animal. It would have helped keep bandages from sticking to wounds. Honey was an ingredient in more Egyptian medicines than any other substance, likely due to its antibacterial qualities. The lint in Egyptian salve drew pus and other fluids out of wounds. The Egyptians often applied lint on its own to cuts to stem bleeding.

"If thou examinest a man having a split in his cheek, shouldst thou find that there is a swelling, protruding and red, on the outside of that split . . . thou shouldst bind it with fresh meat the first day. His treatment is sitting until its swelling is reduced. Thou shalt treat it afterward [with] grease, honey, [and] lint every day until he recovers."

—Edwin Smith Papyrus, ca. 1600 BCE

Egyptian Surgery

Egyptian doctors did little or no major surgery. But they did perform minor surgery such as piercing inflammations on the skin called boils or stitching up battle wounds. The first Egyptian surgeons used knives made from flint, a type of

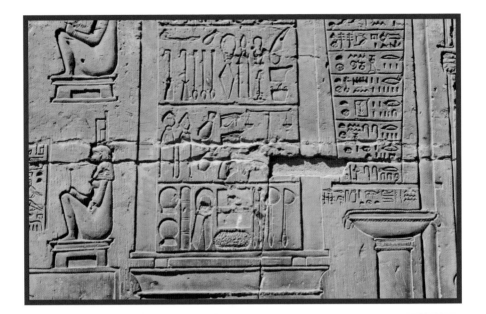

This carving from a temple in Aswan, Egypt, shows ancient medical instruments, including tweezerlike forceps and scales for weighing medicine. The temple dates to 180 BCE.

stone, or obsidian, a kind of glass. These tools were razor sharp. Surgeons also used sharp blades made from the stems of dried reeds. By 1500 BCE, Egyptian surgeons were using metal knives and other surgical tools.

Toothists

Egypt is a dry, sandy place. In ancient Egypt, sand blew into food and often got into people's mouths. The sand acted like sandpaper. It wore away the hard coating of enamel on people's teeth and exposed the teeth's inner nerves and blood vessels.

Studies of mummies show that tooth decay became a bigger and bigger problem as Egyptian society grew. As

This panel is one of six in the tomb of Hesire, a high official of King Zoser of Egypt. Hesire was the Chief of Dentists and Physicians, and the panel shows many of the tools he used in his profession.

farming and trade increased in ancient Egypt, people ate a greater variety of foods, including more sweets, which led to more tooth decay.

Dentists were important in ancient Egypt. Egyptian dentists applied medicines to teeth to slow or stop decay. They did not pull unhealthy teeth. Egyptian dentists tried to keep loose adult teeth from falling out by wrapping pieces of fine gold wire around loose teeth. They fastened the wire to other teeth to hold it in place.

Fresh Breath, Egyptian Style

In modern times, some toothpastes contain baking soda to help clean the teeth and freshen the breath. Egyptians used baking soda more than four thousand years ago. To sweeten their breath, they chewed lumps of natron. This natural salt contains baking soda. It is found throughout Egypt.

The Egyptians also used mouth rinses, much like modern mouthwashes. One popular rinse was made of frankincense, goose fat, cumin, honey, and water. They cleaned their teeth with frayed twigs called chew sticks. They had a shredded end that acted as a brush and a pointed end used as a toothpick. Studies have shown that chew sticks can be more effective than modern toothbrushes.

Treatments That Worked and Treatments That Didn't

The ancient Egyptians used drugs made from plants and animals. They used castor oil, from castor beans, as a laxative. They used gel from aloe plants to treat skin conditions. They drank a tea made from pomegranate bark to kill parasitic worms. These remedies were all effective. Modern people still use them.

But many medicines and treatments from ancient Egypt did not work. For instance, the Egyptians used dead mice in

Medicine in Mesopotamia

East of Egypt, several ancient cultures flourished between the Tigris and Euphrates Rivers. This region is called Mesopotamia and covers parts of present-day Kuwait, Iraq, Syria, and Turkey.

Archaeologists have not found many writings about medicine from the ancient peoples of Mesopotamia. But that does not mean that ancient Mesopotamians did not treat people who were ill. When people got sick, they often sought out an ašipu, or someone who practices religious medicine. An ašipu would determine what angry god or spirit had caused sickness. They then used charms and magic spells to make people well.

Sick people in ancient Mesopotamia could also visit an asu, or a physician. Asus performed minor surgery, such as cutting into wounds to drain pus. They also prescribed remedies made from plants. While there were no hospitals in ancient Mesopotamia, asus did have beds at their offices where patients could be treated or recover from surgery.

One common treatment for injury in ancient Mesopotamia was a plaster. To make a plaster, the asu combined healing ingredients such as plants, spices, honey, and animal fat. The asu then applied the mixture to a cloth. They wrapped it around the patient's injury. Modern studies show that some ancient Mesopotamian plasters might have been effective in keeping wounds clean.

Some natural remedies such as castor oil, pictured here with the beans from which it is derived, are still used today. In modern times, it is commonly used as a laxative and as a treatment for skin problems.

medicines for toothaches, earaches, and other conditions. Did the dead mouse treatments work? Probably not. They might have even made the patient sicker.

Ancient Egyptian physicians developed the first-known treatment for baldness. The Ebers Papyrus called for mixing the fat from several animals and applying the mixture to a bald person's head. Chances are that this treatment didn't work either.

From Balsam to Balm

In modern times, we use spices to liven up our food. We burn incense to make our homes smell good or to mask bad smells.

We wear perfume to make our bodies smell good. People in ancient Egypt used spices, incense, and perfumes for these purposes. But they also used them as medicine.

Balsam is a fragrant, oily substance that flows from balsam fir trees and other plants. People in Egypt used balsam to treat colds and coughs. The modern word balm, which refers to a healing ointment, comes from the Latin word for "balsam." A region called Gilead, in modern-day Jordan, was famous for its balsam fir trees and healing balms. One was known as the Balm of Gilead.

The ancient Egyptians imported vast quantities of myrrh from the Arabian Peninsula. Myrrh comes from the resin of myrrh trees. Egyptians used this pleasant-smelling substance in wound salves. Modern doctors know that myrrh is a mild antibiotic—a substance that slows down or stops the growth of bacteria. People today still use the Balm of Gilead to soothe the skin and relieve pain.

The famous balm of Gilead was balsam from balsam trees, much like this one in modern-day Jordan. Ancient peoples used balsam to treat colds and coughs.

CHAPTER THREE
Ancient India

People in India first established cities in about 2500 BCE. They settled in the valley along the Indus River in modern-day Pakistan and western India. Around 1500 BCE, people from central Asia moved south into India. People in India developed some of the most advanced medical technology of the ancient world.

Knowledge of Life

Ancient Indian medicine was called Ayurveda. This term means "science of life" or "knowledge of life." The Sanskrit word for physician was *vaidya*, or "one who has wisdom."

Much of our knowledge about ancient Indian medicine comes from two books: the *Charaka Samhita* and the *Sushruta Samhita*. The *Charaka Samhita* might date to around 300 BCE. The *Sushruta Samhita* was likely written around 100 CE. Both books provide extensive information on diseases, remedies, childbirth, and other medical issues. They also offer advice on healthy living. The books explain the benefits of a good diet,

The *Sushruta Samhita* was written on palm leaves. The text is considered the foundation of medical practice in India, and remains one of the medical field's most important writings about surgical procedures.

lots of sleep, cleanliness, and exercise. The *Sushruta Samhita* gives detailed information on surgical treatments.

Plastic Surgery

Plastic surgery might seem like modern technology. But Indian doctors performed plastic surgery several thousand years ago. The *Sushruta Samhita* describes how a surgeon might use a flap of skin to create a new nose for someone who lost theirs in battle or as a punishment for a crime.

People in ancient India pierced their ears and stretched

The ancient Indian practice of plugging and stretching the earlobes continues into modern times.

their earlobes into long loops. Then they hung ornaments from the openings. Sometimes the heavy earrings tore people's earlobes. Ancient Indian surgeons learned to repair the damage. Like a nose operation, it involved using a flap of skin from below the ear to create a new earlobe.

Ant Stitches

Indian surgeons sometimes encountered badly wounded patients, such as soldiers wounded in battle. Patients might arrive with a bloody stomach wound. If internal organs, such as the intestines, were cut open, the surgeon had to repair them. The normal procedure was to stitch the intestines using cotton, linen, silk, or another kind of thread. But the operation was dangerous. Traditional cloth stitches absorbed bacteria and could easily get infected.

To protect against infection, ancient Indian surgeons developed a clever solution. Before starting intestinal surgery, they collected giant black ants. Some were almost 1 inch (2.5 cm) long. These insects clamp their powerful jaws around food, their animal enemies, or almost any other object they touch.

After operating on someone's intestines, a surgeon carefully held an ant at the edge of the incision and let it clamp down. The ant's jaws drew the torn edges of the intestines together. The surgeon placed ants along the wound until ant jaws sealed the entire incision. Even after the surgeon cut away the ants' bodies, the jaws stayed firmly clamped in place.

After using the ant stitches, surgeons would replace the intestines in the body and sew up the patient's muscles and

A Good Grasp

Indian toolmakers crafted forceps to look like the jaws of certain animals. The lion forceps had huge jaws. It was good for grasping big structures such as bones. The heron mouth forceps had long, narrow, sharply pointed jaws. Doctors used it to remove splinters and other objects from deep within wounds. Other ancient Indian forceps looked like the jaws of jackals, cats, blue jays, hawks, and crocodiles.

Without quick and proper treatment, a human can die in as few as 15 minutes from the bite of a King Cobra.

skin with ordinary cloth stitches. Within a few weeks, the patient's body would break down the ant jaws. By then the intestines were safely healed.

Snakebite

India is home to many poisonous snakes, including the deadly hooded cobra. In ancient India, vaidyas were skilled in treating bites of poisonous snakes. But they had to act quickly.

If the victim had been bitten on the leg—the most common spot—the vaidya tied a strip of cloth tightly around the leg, about 2 inches (5 cm) above the wound. This helped keep the snake venom from spreading up the leg and into the rest of the body. Then, with a piece of linen cloth in their mouth, the vaidya sucked on the bite. The vaidya drew poison from the wound into the cloth. Next, they cut into the wound with a small knife and cauterized it with a hot coal. Finally, the vaidya applied a healing plaster to the wound.

Fighting Smallpox

Often in history, smallpox has swept through large regions. This disease, caused by a virus, has killed hundreds of millions of people and has scarred or blinded many others.

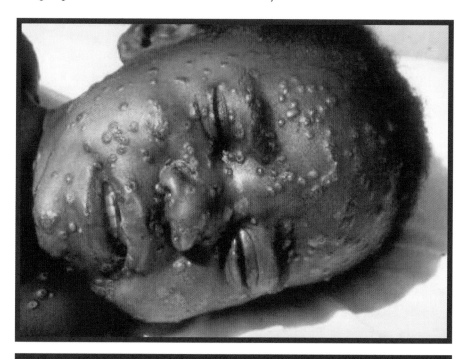

In addition to a painful rash, smallpox symptoms also include a high fever, body aches, and severe fatigue.

Smallpox victims get a rash on the face and other parts of the body. At first the rash looks like thousands of small pimples. Then the pimples become larger and fill with pus. They break open and form crusty scabs. The patient is left with pitted scars, or pocks. Smallpox was so common in some ancient societies that people stood out if their faces did not have pocks. After getting smallpox once, people develop lifelong immunity to the disease.

Ancient Indians may have protected people from smallpox using a technique called variolation. According to ancient Sanskrit texts, doctors took dried scabs from patients with mild cases of smallpox. They then exposed healthy people to the smallpox virus by placing the scabs on their skin or inside their noses or mouths. The exposure made the people sick but usually did not kill them. After that, the patients had lifelong immunity to smallpox. But sometimes, people got severe cases of smallpox after variolation and died.

The First Hospitals

In many ancient societies, sick people remained at home. Sometimes healers or doctors visited them. Sometimes family members treated them. But some ancient civilizations set up hospitals to care for people. In India, for instance, writing carved into a slab of rock around 226 BCE honored the Indian ruler Ashoka. It praised him for building hospitals. Other records indicate that hospitals operated in Sri Lanka, an island off the southern coast of India, around 437 BCE.

These ancient carvings show people praising Ashoka for building hospitals. Many medical facilities in modern India are named for the ruler.

CHAPTER FOUR
Ancient China

People in ancient China began farming between 5000 and 3000 BCE. The first farming villages were in the Yellow River valley in northern China. Gradually, the villages grew into big cities. The Yellow River provided water for drinking, irrigation, and transportation. People also caught fish in the river. When the river flooded the land, it left behind layers of rich yellow soil. The soil was perfect for growing crops.

Magicians and Physicians

Physicians were practicing their trade in China as early as 2000 BCE. They learned to diagnose disease by taking a patient's pulse, observing their skin color, and smelling their breath. They treated illness with herbal remedies, special diets, and massage. They also employed magic spells and charms. Around 500 BCE, the Chinese philosopher Confucius wrote, "A man without persistence will never make a good magician or a good physician."

Chinese physicians like the one shown here used Huangdi's *Nei Ching* to make a diagnosis based on the patient's pulse.

Huangdi's Classic

Much of our knowledge about ancient Chinese medicine comes from the *Nei Ching*. It may be the world's oldest known medical book. In this book, the character Huangdi, often called the Yellow Emperor in English, talks with his prime minister, Qibo. They discuss many aspects of human health and healing. These include human anatomy, disease, and physiology.

Huangdi is a mysterious figure in Chinese history. Nobody knows exactly when he lived or whether he was real or legendary. Some historians think he would have lived

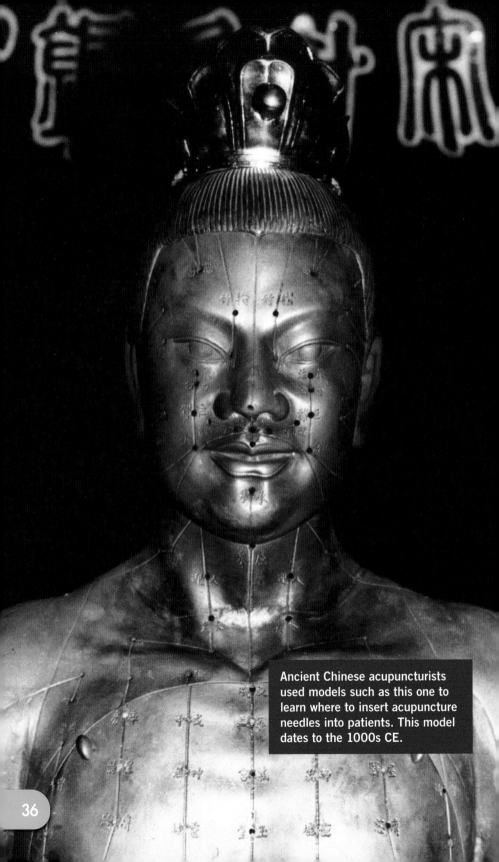

Ancient Chinese acupuncturists used models such as this one to learn where to insert acupuncture needles into patients. This model dates to the 1000s CE.

around 2600 BCE. Historians date the *Nei Ching* to between 479 and 300 BCE. It was likely written long after his death.

The *Nei Ching* explains that good health is based on a balance of two life forces, yin and yang. Yin is a dark, wet, feminine force. Yang is a bright, dry, masculine force. These forces flow through the body along fourteen meridians, or channels. Sickness and pain result when yin and yang are out of balance. The *Nei Ching* tells how to restore this balance using acupuncture. An acupuncturist inserts needles at various points along the body's meridians. The treatments balance yin and yang.

The *Nei Ching* also describes a technique called moxibustion. This treatment involves burning small piles of an herb called moxa on a patient's skin. The process is meant to increase the flow of warmth, blood, and energy inside the body and alleviate certain illnesses.

The *Nei Ching* offers advice on diet. It says, "If too much salt is used for food, the pulse hardens," meaning that someone who oversalts their food may develop high blood pressure. Modern doctors know that eating a lot of salt can raise blood pressure. And high blood pressure increases a person's risk for heart attack and stroke.

Specialists Abound

Like ancient Egypt, ancient China had medical specialists. A book called the *Zhouli* describes the Chinese government during the Zhou dynasty (1046–256 BCE).

The *Zhouli* lists the Zhou emperor's staff. Staff members included a chief of physicians, food physicians (dietitians), physicians for simple diseases, ulcer physicians, and animal

More About Acupuncture

No one knows when acupuncture began in China. Archaeologists have found thin stone needles in ancient Chinese tombs. These might have been used to lance boils. Or they might have been acupuncture needles.

By the time of Huangdi, acupuncture was a fully developed system of medicine in China. Instead of stone needles, Chinese acupuncturists used gold, silver, or bronze needles. In the following centuries, acupuncture became more and more systematic. Chinese doctors wrote many books on acupuncture, moxibustion, and the underlying philosophy of yin and yang.

physicians (veterinarians). The book explains, "All the people belonging to the administration of the kingdom [the emperor's staff], who suffer from ordinary diseases, head diseases, or wounds, come to him [the chief of physicians]. Thereupon he orders the various physicians to share among them the treatment of these diseases." The physicians for simple diseases dealt with common ailments such as headaches, fevers, colds, and coughs. Physicians for ulcers handled more complicated matters such as wounds and internal bleeding.

CHAPTER FIVE

The Ancient Americas

ncient America was home to thousands of different cultures. People lived in the far north, near the North Pole, all the way down to the southernmost tip of South America. Some ancient Americans were hunter-gatherers. Others were farmers or city dwellers.

Like other ancient peoples, ancient Americans used some commonsense methods for maintaining good health. Many groups built sweathouses or sweat lodges. In these small huts, people built fires and heated rocks. They splashed water on the hot rocks to create steam. Sitting and sweating inside a sweathouse refreshed people both physically and mentally. Some peoples, like the Hopi in what is now the southwestern United States, also used massage to treat aches and pains.

The American Medicine Cabinet

Each Indigenous nation used its own plant remedies. The ingredients depended on what grew in the region. Alder trees are common in North America. The Penobscot, who live in

39

Many Indigenous cultures in North America continued to practice ancient medical traditions even as new technology developed. For instance, Hupa people in California built this ancient-style sweathouse, photographed in the early 1920s.

modern-day Maine, drank alder bark tea for stomach cramps. The Potawatomi of the Great Lakes region rubbed alder bark juice on their skin to relieve itching. The nearby Menominee used alder bark to reduce swelling. Other North American nations used alder berries to treat fever and diarrhea. The Cherokee, Blackfoot, Iroquois, and others chewed or made tea from bark of the white willow tree to relieve pain and fevers. The tree's bark contains a substance similar to aspirin.

Sassafras trees, which grow in what is now the eastern United States, provided more medicines. Indigenous peoples

Alder trees such as this one gave ancient North Americans many different remedies. People used alder bark to treat stomach cramps, swelling, and skin problems. Alder berries treated fever and diarrhea.

used sassafras root to treat fevers, sassafras leaves for bruises, and sassafras berries for pain. Many nations used balsam to treat colds, coughs, and asthma. Some used cedar bark for headaches and muscle aches. Slippery elm trees provided a remedy for indigestion. Goldenseal root was good for sore eyes. Witch hazel trees offered remedies for bruises, sprains, and skin problems.

The Healer's Art

Along with plant remedies, ancient American healers used other treatments. Bloodletting was a common practice in the ancient Americas and elsewhere. Doctors made a small cut in a vein or artery in the patient's arm or neck and let some of their blood flow out. They thought it would cure a patient by removing "bad blood." Cauterization was also widespread in the ancient world. Doctors burned wounds to stop their bleeding. Some used cauterization to treat body pains.

Indigenous healers were skilled in setting broken bones. They packed cloth or wet clay around a broken limb before

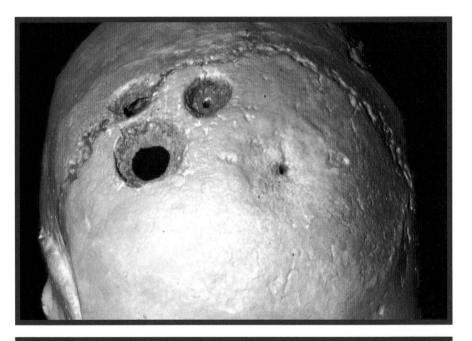

Trephination, shown here, was another method of releasing evil spirits. The practice involved drilling a hole in the skull to allow the spirits to exit the body.

applying a splint. This extra padding helped support the broken bone as it healed. The Ojibwe people of the northern Great Lakes region used cedar wood to make splints. The Pima of modern-day Arizona made splints from the ribs of giant cactuses.

Magic and Medicine

In many Indigenous societies, disease and medicine were intertwined with the spirit world. People thought that witches, spirits, and evil spells caused illness and other misfortunes. So ancient American healers had to be skilled in several ways. They had to know how to use medicines and other remedies. But they also had to communicate with spirits to cure or prevent illness.

When someone got sick and blamed evil spirits, the shaman used magic to chase the spirits away. Sometimes they tried to suck the spirits from the patient's body with a hollow animal bone, a stone, or a reed. This sometimes worked. That's because the shaman sucked out pus, infected tissue, or snake venom from the patient's body. Removing infection or venom could help the sick person recover.

Ancient Indigenous doctors used smooth stones to grind up plants to make medicine. They used syringes made from hollow bones and animal bladders to inject medicine into patients. Healers often played drums and rattles to communicate with the spirit world. They sometimes wore masks and costumes to frighten away evil spirits. Some doctors carried a medicine bundle made of animal skins. The bundle held charms and magical objects, such as deer tails and snake bones.

Plagues from the East

Cinchona trees grow on the eastern slopes of the Andes Mountains in South America. The bark of these trees contains a medicine called quinine. The Indigenous Quechua, Cañari, and Chimú peoples ground the bark into powder. They mixed it in hot water to make medicine to reduce fevers.

When Europeans came to South America in the 1500s,

A book called the *Codex de la Cruz-Badiano*, created by Spanish explorers, lists and illustrates hundreds of medicinal plants used by the Aztecs of Mexico. The book dates to 1552.

they brought diseases that people of the Americas had not been exposed to before. One of these diseases was malaria. Malaria makes people feverish and, if left untreated, can result in kidney failure, seizures, and death. When this new disease arrived in their area, the local Indigenous peoples naturally turned to cinchona bark, which they knew to be effective in treating fevers. As it turned out, quinine in the bark was a powerful treatment for malaria. This discovery was a major breakthrough for Europeans, who had no effective malaria drugs in their homelands. Europeans shipped the bark back to Europe in large quantities.

Malaria was not the only disease that Europeans brought to the Americas. European explorers, settlers, and soldiers also brought smallpox, measles, typhus, diphtheria, mumps, tuberculosis, and yellow fever. Because Indigenous peoples hadn't been exposed to these diseases, their bodies did not have any immunity against them. Epidemics of smallpox and other diseases killed Indigenous people by the hundreds and sometimes by the thousands. Some historians think that diseases from Europe wiped out about 90 percent of the Indigenous population in the Americas.

CHAPTER SIX
Ancient Greece

Ancient Greece was a center of learning in the ancient world. Not surprisingly, ancient Greece was also home to skilled doctors. Many modern medical traditions have their roots in ancient Greece.

The God of Medicine

As in many ancient societies, medicine and religion were closely connected in ancient Greece. People thought that gods could cause and cure illness. The Greeks worshipped a god of healing named Asclepius. They prayed to him when they got sick or when epidemics swept through Greek cities. According to Greek myth, Asclepius learned the art of healing from his father, the god Apollo. Asclepius's symbol was a snake coiled around a staff. The staff of Asclepius continues to be a symbol of medicine and health care in modern times.

The ancient Greeks built temples to honor Asclepius. The temples were part health spa, part house of worship. Sick people went there to pray to Asclepius and be cured. Priests

This marble carving from the fourth century BCE shows Asclepius caring for a patient.

at the temples treated patients with special diets, massage, and plant-based medicines. The health temples were usually built near mineral springs, where mineral-rich water flowed from underground. People believed that bathing in or drinking the waters would cure illness. The temple to Asclepius in Pergamum, in modern-day Turkey, had a mineral spring at its center. One Roman writer described the curative powers of the water there: "For many who have bathed in it recovered their eyesight, while many by drinking were cured of chest ailments and regained vital breathing. For in some cases it cured their feet, while for others it cured some other part of the body." No doubt, soaking in the mineral waters relieved people's aches and pains. But stories of miracle cures were most likely exaggerated.

The Father of Medicine

Hippocrates was a physician and a teacher of medicine in ancient Greece. Hippocrates was born around 460 BCE on the Greek island of Cos. The island had a temple to honor Asclepius.

Hippocrates was one of the first physicians to diagnose diseases of the heart and lungs, as well as the first to recognize that some illnesses are chronic while others are acute, or temporary.

What Kind of Plague?

The Great Plague of Athens struck Greece around 430 BCE. The plague killed up to three hundred thousand people in Greece, about 25 percent of the population. In his book *The History of the Peloponnesian War*, the Greek historian Thucydides described the plague. He said that victims suddenly got high fevers and sore throats. Blisters broke out on their skin. They vomited, had diarrhea, and suffered from intense thirst. Some victims developed hiccups that would not stop.

The bubonic plague is caused by the bacterium *Yersinia pestis*. This disease struck the people of Constantinople in 542 CE and ravaged medieval Europe. But the Great Plague of Athens was not necessarily caused by *Yersinia pestis*. Ancient writers often used the term plague to describe any widespread epidemic. The epidemic in Athens might have been the bubonic plague, or it might have been caused by another disease.

In 1996 researchers in California theorized that the Great Plague of Athens was an Ebola outbreak. Ebola caused alarm in 1995 when it killed 242 people in what is now the Democratic Republic of the Congo in Africa. The researchers said that Ebola symptoms and the plague symptoms Thucydides reported were very similar. They noted that African green monkeys transmit the Ebola virus to humans. Near Athens, archaeologists had found ancient wall paintings showing African green monkeys. Traders must have brought the monkeys with them after traveling to Africa. Perhaps the monkeys brought Ebola to Athens. Not all scientists agreed with the Ebola theory. One critique was that Thucydides's medical descriptions were imprecise and couldn't be counted on as solid evidence.

In 2006 Greek researchers studied human remains from an ancient burial pit in Athens dating back to the Great Plague. The researchers analyzed the teeth of some of the skeletons and found evidence that typhoid fever had killed the plague victims. But scientists argued that typhoid was too common to be the cause of the plague. The puzzle of the Great Plague of Athens remains a topic of debate among both scientists and historians.

Hippocrates established a school as part of the temple complex. He taught medical students to carefully observe each patient's symptoms and select an appropriate treatment. His contributions to medicine later earned him the title the Father of Medicine.

Of all Hippocrates's contributions to medicine, the use of case histories might be the most important. Hippocrates kept a case history on each patient. He described the patient's symptoms, his own diagnosis, the treatment he prescribed, and the outcome of the treatment.

Hippocrates and other ancient Greek doctors treated patients with plant remedies, wound dressings, and minor surgery. But they did not know enough about the workings of the human body to treat serious illnesses. They did not know about germs or how to keep wounds from becoming infected. They did not know much about how organs worked. Although Hippocrates took a scientific approach to medicine, his knowledge was limited.

Hippocratic Oath

Legend says that Hippocrates made his students take a pledge.

They had to promise to practice medicine in an ethical way. Many ancient Greek doctors took such an oath. It's called the Hippocratic oath, although Hippocrates probably didn't write it. In the oath, ancient Greek doctors swore to use medicine for good and not for harm. They promised never to give a poisonous drug to a patient. They also promised to respect patients' privacy. Modern doctors take a similar oath.

"To Cut Up"

Our modern medical term *anatomy* comes from ancient Greek words that mean "to cut up." The study of human anatomy involves dissecting, or cutting up, dead bodies. Doctors must know how the body is put together to diagnose and treat diseases.

"I swear by Apollo the physician, and by Asklepios . . . and all the gods and goddesses, and call them to witness that . . . I will prescribe treatments to the best of my ability and judgement for the good of the sick, and never for a harmful or illicit [unlawful] purpose."

—Hippocratic oath excerpt, ca. 500s BCE

The ancient Greeks laid the groundwork for this key area of medical science. In the 500s BCE, Alcmaeon was the first person ever recorded to have dissected part of a human body for scientific study. He wrote descriptions of the optic nerve in the human eye and the eustachian tube inside the ear.

The Greek physician Herophilos (ca. 335–280 BCE) was another anatomy pioneer. He regularly dissected human bodies for scientific study. Because of this, he is known as the father of anatomy. He started a medical school in Alexandria, Egypt. Although not officially part of Greece, this city was

Treating the Mind

People in the ancient world did not know much about mental illness. Many people thought that witches or evil spirits caused mental illness. Some societies locked up people with mental health issues and treated them cruelly. Around 100 BCE, a Greek physician named Asclepiades took a new approach to mental illness. He urged humane treatments for mentally ill people. He treated them with special diets and warm baths. He even used music to calm upset patients. Asclepiades was ahead of his time. It wasn't until the twentieth century that health care embraced humane treatment for those with mental illnesses.

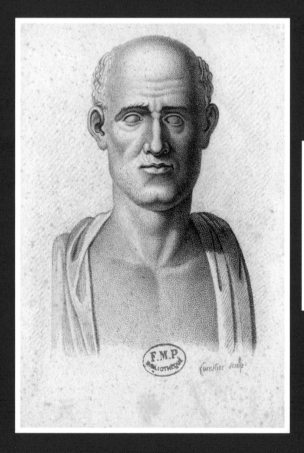

Often called the Father of Psychiatry, Asclepiades treated mental illness as a health issue. His gentle methods of treatment included music therapy, which is still used in modern times.

These pictures were carved on the wall of a temple built to honor Asclepius, the Greek god of healing. Scalpels are shown in the center. The objects on each side of the scalpels are cupping glasses. Ancient doctors used the glasses to draw blood from the body.

home to many ancient Greek scholars and scientists. At Alexandria, Herophilos wrote the first detailed description of the human brain. He also recognized the difference between arteries, which carry fresh, oxygen-rich blood away from the heart, and veins, which carry blood from body tissues back to the heart.

The Pus Puller

Few medical devices are more important than the syringe. It consists of a hollow tube with a plunger. Doctors and nurses attach these syringes to a hollow needle and use them to inject medicine, take blood samples, and drain fluid from the body. Early peoples in many cultures made syringes out of hollow bones and animal bladders. The ancient Greeks used similar devices made from animal bladders and thin metal pipes.

Ctesibius, a Greek engineer from Alexandria, invented a new kind of syringe around 280 BCE. It was made of two pieces of metal: a piston, or sliding valve, and a hollow cylinder. The cylinder tapered to a point at one end. Pushing on the piston forced air or liquid inside the cylinder to squirt out at the pointed end. Drawing back on the piston sucked material from wounds or body cavities. The first description of the cylinder-and-piston syringe appears in a book written in the first century CE.

The ancient Greeks used syringes mostly to suck pus out of pimples, boils, and infected wounds. The Greek name for the syringe, *pyulkos*, means "pus puller."

Dissections helped improve ancient Greek medical knowledge. By studying anatomy, ancient Greek surgeons learned to do major surgery. They learned how to safely amputate limbs, repair hernias, and remove stones from the bladder.

The Four Humors

Like the ancient Chinese, the ancient Greeks thought that sickness resulted when the body was out of balance. Greek physicians thought that four humors, or fluids, controlled human health. These humors were phlegm, blood, yellow bile, and black bile. The fluids were part of a larger philosophy, or belief system. In this philosophy, each of the four humors was associated with a different natural substance, a specific moisture and temperature, a certain part of the body, and a certain season of the year. The associations were as follows:

Humor	Natural substance	Moisture and temperature	Body part	Season
Phlegm	Water	Wet and cold	Brain	Winter
Blood	Air	Wet and hot	Blood	Spring
Yellow bile	Fire	Dry and hot	Liver	Summer
Black bile	Earth	Dry and cold	Spleen	Autumn

The ancient Greek physician's job was to balance the humors. Suppose a patient had a fever. Their body was hot and dry. The physician would understand this as the patient having too much yellow bile. The physician would try to restore balance by increasing the patient's phlegm, which was wet and cold—the opposite of hot and dry. The physician might prescribe a cold bath.

Often ancient Greek physicians tried to rid patients of excessive humors. Physicians cut and bled patients to rid them of too much blood. They often prescribed medicine made of hellebore, a poisonous plant. The medicine caused any number of severe reactions, including sneezing, vomiting, diarrhea, and muscle cramps. Ancient Greek physicians thought these reactions were beneficial. Through purging, physicians thought, patients would rid themselves of the excess humors that made them sick. But hellebore made patients sicker. Sometimes, it even killed them.

CHAPTER SEVEN

Ancient Rome

Ancient Rome began as a small city in the 700s BCE. Over the following centuries, the ancient Romans built a great empire based in modern-day Italy. By the first century CE, the empire reached into central Europe, the Middle East, and northern Africa.

The Romans conquered other countries and adopted foreign technology, including medical technology. Rome embraced a significant amount of technology from ancient Greece. According to one ancient writer, Rome was "swept along on the puffs of the clever brains of Greece."

Historians think the Romans also adopted medical knowledge from ancient India. The ancient Romans and ancient Indians often traded with each other. Roman traders brought back medicines and information about surgical procedures from India. One Roman historian complained that people ignored medicinal plants growing around their own country because so many effective medicines from India already existed.

On Medicine

Aulus Cornelius Celsus was a wealthy Roman landowner who lived during the first century CE. Celsus wrote a long book on warfare, farming, medicine, science, law, and philosophy. The medical chapter was called "De Medicina," or "On Medicine." It described diseases, treatments, special diets, surgery, and other medical topics.

"De Medicina" provided accurate descriptions of many medical terms. Doctors around the world still diagnose inflammation using Celsus's four basic signs: redness, swelling, heat, and pain.

The Romans took advantage of medical technology developed in other empires. This fresco shows the ancient Roman port of Stabiae, where merchants unloaded ships full of medicines and other goods from India. This art is at a museum in Naples, Italy.

To Cut Up, Continued

The ancient study of anatomy that began with Herophilos in Greece continued with Galen in the Roman period. Galen was born in Pergamum, in modern-day Turkey, in 129 CE. Galen studied medicine in Alexandria before returning to Pergamum, where he learned a great deal about wounds and the human body by treating wounded gladiators.

In 162 CE, Galen moved to Rome. He became the physician to Emperor Marcus Aurelius and his family. Along with this job, Galen continued his own medical research and writing. He learned more about anatomy by dissecting animals and studying human skeletons.

Galen put all his knowledge into a sixteen-volume book called *On Anatomical Procedures*. It is considered one of the most important early writings on human anatomy.

Taking Your Pulse

As part of a medical examination, Galen would take a patient's pulse. Doctors often feel a patient's pulse in their wrist. The pulse mirrors the pumping action of the person's heart. Galen noted that if the pulse is too fast, too slow, or irregular, it may indicate heart disease.

The Cesarean Section

During childbirth, some babies cannot pass through the birth canal safely. Then doctors must perform a cesarean section. Doctors make an incision into the parent's abdomen and uterus to remove the baby.

Many people think the term *cesarean* originated from the surgical birth of Julius Caesar. He was Rome's dictator from 46 to 44 BCE. But medical historians think that it's unlikely Caesar was born by cesarean section. At the time of Caesar's birth, Roman doctors only performed the operation when the birthing parent was dying or dead and therefore could not push the baby out. But Julius Caesar's mother was alive long after his birth. The word *cesarean* may come from another Latin word, *caedare*, which means "to cut open."

Cesarean sections were probably performed long before Roman times. Ancient Indian and Egyptian writings mention surgical births. One ancient Chinese picture shows the operation.

Ancient Eye Surgery

Indian surgeons probably invented cataract surgery. Historians think the Romans learned about the technology from Indian doctors or from Indian medical books.

Ancient doctors performed the surgery with a fine needle. They inserted the needle into a patient's eye. They carefully

Galen's Legacy

Galen wrote about more than five hundred medicines derived from plants. He often mixed plant medicines together in complicated prescriptions. Some mixtures contained dozens of ingredients. In modern times, physicians use the term *galenical preparations* to describe drugs made from plants.

pushed the clouded lens to the bottom of the eyeball. Celsus knew the danger of this procedure. If the needle slipped and touched the retina, the tissue-thin membrane at the back of the eye, the patient would be blinded. Celsus advised doctors to tie down their patient or to have a strong assistant hold the patient still, so that they didn't move during the operation.

When modern doctors perform cataract surgery, they remove the clouded lens from the eye and replace it with an artificial lens. Sometimes cataract patients must wear contact lenses or eyeglasses after the surgery to see clearly. Ancient doctors did not replace clouded lenses with artificial lenses. Ancient peoples also did not have eyeglasses or contact lenses. A patient's vision would have been badly blurred after cataract surgery in ancient times. But they would still have seen better than they did before the surgery.

This decoration on a second century CE Roman tomb shows a physician examining a patient's eyes. This part of the tomb is at a museum in Ravenna, Italy.

Preserved in Ash

Archaeologists have found hundreds of ancient Roman surgical instruments. These instruments were made with great precision. For example, Roman forceps were high-quality metal tools. Their jaws aligned precisely and closed tightly when grasping. Medical historians note that Roman surgical instruments were much better than the instruments available to surgeons during the Renaissance more than one thousand years later.

Archaeologists have found many surgical instruments in the remains of Pompeii. This ancient Roman city was destroyed when Mount Vesuvius, a volcano, erupted in 79 CE. The eruption rained poisonous gases, cinders, and hot ash down on the city. The ash later cooled and hardened around people's bodies and other objects. Archaeologists have found ancient Roman medical kits preserved inside hardened shells of ash. The kits consisted of hollow, pocket-sized metal cylinders with probes, scalpels, and other medical tools inside.

Sanitation

Many of Rome's most important advances in medical technology did not involve the treatment of disease. They involved disease prevention through sanitation and public health measures. One of the most important sanitation measures in ancient Rome was sewage disposal. Every street in the city of Rome had a sewer running along its length. The homes of wealthy people had indoor toilets. Pipes carried human waste directly from these toilets into city sewers. Less wealthy people used chamber pots and emptied them into sewers themselves.

Water flowed continuously through each sewer. The

Ancient OB-GYN

Women were often doctors in ancient Rome. Most of them focused on diseases specific to women. A *medica a mammis* was a woman doctor who specialized in breast health. *Obstretrices* were midwives. They cared for pregnant patients and delivered babies.

water emptied into larger and larger channels. Eventually, all the sewers in Rome emptied into the Cloaca Maxima, or "Greatest Sewer." The Cloaca Maxima emptied into the Tiber River.

Pure Water

Rome's sewer system had one big drawback. Sewage emptying into the Tiber River polluted the water. Thousands of people got sick from drinking polluted river water. People in ancient Rome needed a source of clean drinking water.

Rome solved the problem by building its famous aqueduct system. Aqueducts carried clean water from springs or lakes in the countryside into the city of Rome. Some aqueducts were elevated. Others were underground. All Roman aqueducts were built with a slight slope so that water flowed toward the city.

The Hospital System

At its height, the Roman Empire controlled a vast territory. The

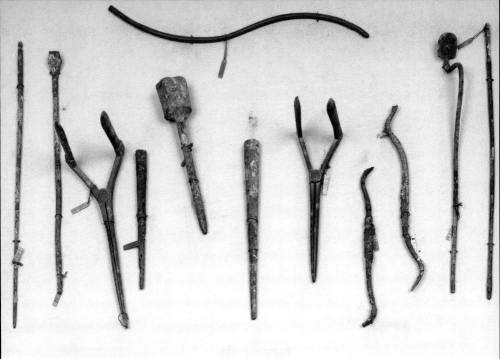

These surgical instruments—including probes and forceps—were used in the ancient Roman city of Pompeii. A volcanic eruption destroyed the city in 79 CE.

empire stretched from central Europe to northern Africa to the Middle East. Roman legions, or military divisions, fought battles far from home. When a Roman soldier was wounded, he had to be treated quickly. To accomplish this, Romans established a special military medical corps to treat wounded soldiers right on the battlefield. Their doctors and medical assistants also treated soldiers in hospitals called valetudinaria. Most were located near battlefields or in military field camps.

Archaeologists have discovered the ruins of at least twenty-five valetudinaria in the former Roman Empire. Most were built during the 100s and 200s CE. The builders followed a standard plan. In each hospital, small wards opened off a central corridor.

Archaeologists have found the remains of medicines and

medical instruments in the ruins of some ancient Roman military hospitals. In one, archaeologists found seeds of the henbane plant. This plant contains the drug scopolamine. Modern doctors use scopolamine to treat nausea, vomiting, and motion sickness. The drug can also make people drowsy. Roman physicians combined scopolamine with opium. This combination made patients drowsy and relieved their pain.

Roman Barb Puller

Warfare in the Roman Empire was brutal and bloody. Soldiers fought with swords, spears, and arrows. Some spearheads and arrowheads had barbs, or extra points that projected backward. Barbed points were difficult to remove from the body. Pulling them out usually caused more damage because the barbs caught on tissue and tore it.

Roman doctors used a spoonlike instrument to pull barbed arrowheads and spearheads from wounded patients. A doctor inserted the device behind an arrowhead or spearhead and caught the main point in a hole in the bowl of the spoon. The spoon formed a shield around the barb. The doctor could then remove the object without causing further damage.

After the Ancients

Ancient societies rose and fell. Often groups grew politically or economically weak, and stronger groups conquered them. But even after a culture died out, its technology often remained. Conquering groups learned about it from books and by word of mouth. They built on the knowledge of conquered peoples to further develop technology.

This wasn't always so. After the Roman Empire fell to invaders in 476 CE, Europe entered the Middle Ages (about 500 to 1500 CE). During the early Middle Ages, many libraries were destroyed or neglected. Many writings about medicine disappeared. People also forgot about the public health measures used by the ancient Romans. In some European cities, people dumped human and animal waste into city streets. They drank water from polluted rivers. Unsanitary conditions led to many outbreaks of disease.

The medical situation was better in the Middle East during this period. Physicians there still had translations of medical texts written by the ancient Greeks. Middle

65

Ibn Sina, who lived in Persia, wrote an encyclopedia of medicine around 1025 CE.

Eastern doctors operated medical schools, studied anatomy, and improved surgical techniques. In the Persian Empire (based in modern-day Iran), a doctor, Ibn Sina (980–1037 CE), compiled a medical encyclopedia. Called the *Canon of Medicine*, it was the most advanced medical book of the period. It contained descriptions of diseases, medicines, anatomy, physiology, and psychology.

Death and Rebirth

In the 1300s, an epidemic of bubonic plague swept through Europe. Infected people got fevers, headaches, body aches, and painful swellings on parts of their bodies. They usually died within five days. Some people thought the plague was a punishment from God. They didn't know that bacteria caused the plague. They didn't understand how it spread from person to person. Physicians tried all sorts of remedies, but they were nearly powerless to help people who got sick with the plague. By the time the epidemic ended, the "Black Death" had killed between 25 and 50 percent of Europe's population.

On the heels of the Black Death, Europe entered the Renaissance (early 1300s–1600). The era was a time of great artistic, scientific, and intellectual achievement in Europe. During this period, Europeans rediscovered some of the technology and knowledge of ancient Greece and Rome. European doctors once again began to study human anatomy, diseases, and medicines.

Italian scholars found an ancient copy of Celsus's "De Medicina" in the early 1400s. Soon afterward, Johannes Gutenberg of Germany invented the printing press. This machine enabled people to print many copies of a book in a short time. In 1478 scholars reprinted "De Medicina," the first medical book reproduced on the printing press.

The Floodgates of Knowledge

In the 1500s, European medical knowledge began to surpass the knowledge of ancient Greece and Rome. Italian artist and inventor Leonardo da Vinci performed dissections and made drawings of the body parts he saw. A French doctor, Ambroise Paré, studied gunshot wounds and surgical wounds. He determined that wounds healed best when left to heal naturally. He advised against using cauterization. In the early

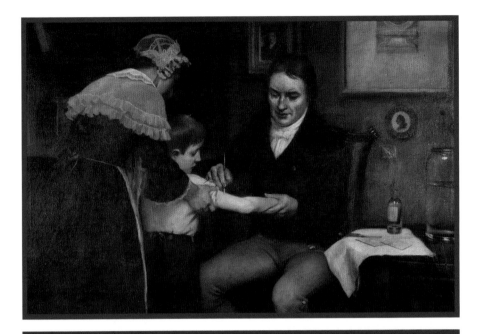

This nineteenth-century painting shows Jenner vaccinating a child. In modern times, vaccination is used to protect people from a variety of diseases.

1600s, English physician William Harvey studied the human circulatory system—the way blood travels throughout the body. He learned about the workings of the heart, the arteries, and the veins. In the late 1700s, British physician Edward Jenner discovered a new way to protect people from smallpox. His procedure, called vaccination, was similar to the ancient Indian practice of variolation but was less likely to cause severe illness.

More breakthroughs followed. In the 1800s, doctors learned how to anesthetize parts of the body, or numb them, before surgery. Using microscopes, doctors identified bacteria and viruses that can cause disease. They devised more vaccinations to prevent more diseases. They discovered how to look inside the body using X-rays.

Around the turn of the twentieth century, governments enacted new public health measures. Big cities in Europe, the United States, and other places installed water and sewage systems. These systems ensured that people had clean water to drink and that wastewater was carried away safely. Public health officials recommended vaccinating children against diseases and advocated good hygiene.

A dramatic medical breakthrough occurred in 1928. That year doctors discovered antibiotics. Doctors used antibiotics to treat people with meningitis, tuberculosis, scarlet fever, and other diseases. Before antibiotics, these diseases were often fatal. After antibiotics, people who got these diseases were usually cured.

The Good Old Days

Many ancient remedies really worked—and still do. In the 400s BCE, ancient Greek doctors prescribed the leaves and bark of the willow tree for pain. Modern doctors know that willow leaves and bark contain salicin. Once inside the human body, this chemical turns into salicylate. Salicylate is the main ingredient in aspirin.

Ancient people devised effective medical technology with the materials and knowledge available to them at the time. While not every treatment or remedy has survived to modern times, much of modern medicine stems from medical understanding and technology that has existed through the ages.

TIMELINE

2600s BCE	Imhotep practices medicine in ancient Egypt.
ca. 2500	Peseshet, the first woman doctor known by name, practices medicine in ancient Egypt.
ca. 1900	Ancient Egyptians write about childbirth and gynecology in the Kahun Papyrus.
ca. 1600	Ancient Egyptians write about surgery and injuries in the Edwin Smith Papyrus.
ca. 1500	Ancient Egyptians write a medical encyclopedia, the Ebers Papyrus.
ca. 600	Construction begins on Rome's sewer system.
500s	Alcmaeon is the first person to dissect human bodies for medical study.
430–425	The Great Plague of Athens strikes Greece, killing one-third to one-half of the Greek population.
400s	Hippocrates teaches medicine on the island of Cos.
400s or 300s	Ancient Chinese write down the *Nei Ching*.
312	The first aqueduct is built in Rome.
300s	Herophilos founds a medical school in Alexandria, Egypt.
ca. 280	Ctesibius of Alexandria invents a cylinder-and-piston syringe.
ca. 100	Asclepiades advocates for humane treatments for people with mental illnesses.
ca. 40–90 CE	Aulus Cornelius Celsus writes "De Medicina." The Indian surgeon Sushruta writes the *Sushruta Samhita*.
100s	Galen practices and studies medicine in Rome. Roman armies build hospitals at military camps.
542	The bubonic plague strikes Constantinople, killing almost half the population.
1300s	The bubonic plague kills up to one-half of Europe's people.
1478	Italian scholars reprint Celsus's "De Medicina."

1500s	Europeans bring new diseases to the Americas. They learn that cinchona bark can be used to treat malaria from the Indigenous peoples of the Andes Mountains.
1996	US scientists propose that the Ebola virus caused the Great Plague of Athens.
2003	Laborers discover the bodies of Old Croghan Man and Clonycavan Man in peat bogs in Ireland.
2006	Greek scientists propose that typhoid fever caused the Great Plague of Athens.

GLOSSARY

acupuncture: a Chinese practice of inserting fine needles into the skin along the body's meridians (energy pathways) to cure disease or relieve pain

antibiotic: a medicine that kills or slows the growth of bacteria

archaeologist: a scientist who studies the remains of past human cultures

bloodletting: drawing blood out of the body to try to cure sickness

cataract: a clouding of the lens of the eye

cauterization: burning the skin to stop bleeding or to heal a wound

dissection: cutting apart a living thing to study its internal structure

epidemic: an outbreak of disease that affects many people in the same region at the same time

forceps: tweezerlike tools used by physicians and dentists for grasping, holding, or pulling at parts of the body

gynecology: the branch of medicine that deals with functions and diseases of the female reproductive system

immunity: resistance to a particular disease

inflammation: a response by the body to injury or infection. Inflammation causes redness, swelling, heat, and pain.

physiology: the study of how the body functions

plague: a widespread outbreak of deadly disease

plaster: a cloth treated with medicine and applied to an injury

plastic surgery: repairing or replacing deformed, damaged, or lost body parts to improve their appearance or function

resin: a sticky substance that comes from the gum or sap of a tree

sanitation: the cleaning or disposing of waterborne waste within a community to promote health

shaman: a person who uses magic and other techniques to cure the sick and communicate with spirits

syringe: a device used to inject fluids into or withdraw fluids from the body

vaccination: injecting someone with a medicine to protect them from severe infection

variolation: an ancient method of giving someone a weakened form of smallpox to make them immune to smallpox

SOURCE NOTES

15   "Chief of Physicians . . . the pyramid builders.": Guido Majno, *The Healing Hand: Man and Wound in the Ancient World* (Cambridge, MA: Harvard University Press, 1991), 73.

16   "in medical knowledge . . . the world behind.": Christos Evangeliou, *Hellenic Philosophy: Origin and Character* (Aldershot, UK: Ashgate, 2006), 12.

17   "the practice of . . . only one disease.": Michael J. O'Dowd, *The History of Medications for Women* (New York: Parthenon, 2001), 49.

19   "If thou examinest . . . until he recovers.": James Henry Breasted, ed., *The Edwin Smith Surgical Papyrus* (Chicago: University of Chicago, 1930), 266.

34   "A man without . . . a good physician.": Paul Ulrich Unschuld, *Medical Ethics in Imperial China: A Study in Historical Anthropology* (Berkeley: University of California Press, 1979), 39.

37   "If too much . . . the pulse hardens.": Song Wan and Anthony P. C. Yim, *Cardiothoracic Surgery in China: Past, Present and Future* (Hong Kong: Chinese University Press, 2007), 210.

38   "All the people . . . of these diseases.": Majno, *Healing Hand*, 237.

47–48 "For many who . . . of the body.": Gerald David Hart, *Asclepius: The God of Medicine* (London: Royal Society of Medicine, 2000), 69.

51   "I swear by . . . illicit [unlawful] purpose.": Jenny Sutcliffe and Nancy Duin, *A History of Medicine* (New York: Barnes and Nobles Books, 1992), 18.

56   "swept along on . . . brains of Greece.": Majno, *Healing Hand*, 341.

SELECTED BIBLIOGRAPHY

Ackerknecht, Erwin H. *A Short History of Medicine*. Baltimore: Johns Hopkins University Press, 1982.

Adkins, Lesley, and Roy A. Adkins. *Handbook to Life in Ancient Rome*. New York: Facts on File, 1994.

Bourke, John G. *Apache Medicine–Men*. New York: Dover, 1993.

Estes, J. Worth. *The Medical Skills of Ancient Egypt*. New York: Science History Publications/USA, 1989.

James, Peter, and Nick Thorpe. *Ancient Inventions*. New York: Ballantine Books, 1994.

Kunow, Marianna Appel. *Maya Medicine: Traditional Healing in Yucatán*. Albuquerque: University of New Mexico Press, 2003.

Majno, Guido. *The Healing Hand: Man and Wound in the Ancient World*. Cambridge, MA: Harvard University Press, 1991.

Nunn, John F. *Ancient Egyptian Medicine*. Norman: University of Oklahoma Press, 1995.

Porter, Roy, ed. *The Cambridge Illustrated History of Medicine*. Cambridge: Cambridge University Press, 1996.

Saggs, H. W. F. *Civilization before Greece and Rome*. New Haven, CT: Yale University Press, 1989.

Salzberg, Hugh W. *From Caveman to Chemist*. Washington, DC: American Chemical Society Press, 1991.

Sigerist, Henry E. *A History of Medicine. Vol. 1: Primitive and Archaic Medicine*. New York: Oxford University Press, 1987.

Starr, Chester G., ed. *A History of the Ancient World*. New York: Oxford University Press, 1991.

Sutcliff, Jenny, and Nancy Duin. *A History of Medicine*. New York: Barnes and Noble Books, 1992.

Vogel, Virgil J. *American Indian Medicine*. Norman: University of Oklahoma Press, 1970.

FURTHER READING

Books

Goldsmith, Connie. *Understanding Coronaviruses: SARS, MERS, and the COVID-19 Pandemic*. Minneapolis: Twenty-First Century Books, 2022.
In 2019 a new strain of coronavirus appeared and quickly spread across the globe. This thoroughly researched book examines the history of coronaviruses and how this novel strain impacted daily life around the world.

Haelle, Tara. *Vaccination Investigation: The History and Science of Vaccines*. Minneapolis: Twenty-First Century Books, 2018.
Learn about the fascinating history of vaccines, their important role in protecting community health, and cutting-edge research.

Rector, Rebecca Kraft. *The Early River Valley Civilizations*. New York: Rosen, 2016.
Early civilizations formed along the banks of rivers where the land was fertile. This book explores the first communities that formed in Mesopotamia, ancient Egypt, the Indus Valley in India, and the Yellow River valley in China.

Terrell, Brandon. *Antibiotics: A Graphic History*. Minneapolis: Graphic Universe, 2022.
In 1929 the accidental discovery of the first antibiotic, penicillin, kicked off a medical revolution. The use of this new treatment has saved countless lives from World War II soldiers to modern hospital patients. Explore current issues in antibiotics and the best ways to fight bacteria in this graphic history.

Woods, Michael, and Mary B. Woods. *Agriculture through the Ages: From Silk to Supermarkets*. Minneapolis: Twenty-First Century Books, 2024.
Humans learned to farm more than twelve thousand years ago. The first farmers used simple technology, but over the centuries and millennia, civilizations invented technology that helped them farm more land and produce more food. Discover how different cultures met their farming needs in this compendium.

Websites

Ayurveda

> https://www.hopkinsmedicine.org/health/wellness-and
> -prevention/ayurveda
> This page, hosted by Johns Hopkins, provides an overview of
> Ayurveda, or traditional Indian medical practice. It also outlines
> the current licensing and standard limitations in the United States.

Aztec Aqueducts

> https://www.history.com/topics/ancient-americas/aztec-aqueducts
> -video
> Romans weren't the only people to build aqueducts. This short
> video describes how the Aztecs designed a sophisticated system
> to provide clean water to their capital city.

Gladys Tantaquidgeon

> https://www.mohegan.nsn.us/about/our-tribal-history
> /in-memoriam/gladys-tantaquidgeon
> Gladys Tantaquidgeon was a Mohegan medicine woman who
> studied anthropology at the University of Pennsylvania in the
> 1920s. Learn more about her life preserving traditional Native
> knowledge, ceremonies, art forms, and stories.

Health and Medicine

> https://americanhistory.si.edu/collections/subjects/health
> -medicine
> The National Museum of American History hosts a collection of
> medical science artifacts, ranging from bloodletting instruments
> to the first artificial heart implanted in a human. Explore the
> collection online at this web page.

"The Mummy Who Would Be King"

> http://www.pbs.org/wgbh/nova/mummy
> The ancient Egyptians learned a lot about human anatomy by
> preparing mummies for the afterlife. This website, a companion
> to the *Nova* television show of the same name, provides an
> introduction to mummies and mummy making.

INDEX

ABOUT THE AUTHORS

Michael Woods is a science and medical journalist in Washington, DC. He has won many national writing awards. Mary B. Woods is a school librarian. Their past books include the fifteen–volume *Disasters Up Close* series and many titles in the *Seven Wonders* series. The Woodses have four children. When not writing, reading, or enjoying their seven grandchildren, the Woodses travel to gather material for future books.

PHOTO ACKNOWLEDGMENTS

George E. Koronaios/Wikipedia, p. 5; JOSEPH EID/AFP/Getty Images, p. 6; Museum of London/Heritage Images/Getty Images, p. 9; SSPL/Getty Images, p. 10; makasana/Getty Images, p. 11; KeithBinns/Getty Images, p. 12; MPI/Getty Images, p. 13; Jeff Dahl/Wikimedia Commons PD, p. 15; DEA/A. DAGLI ORTI/De Agostini/Getty Images, p. 16; DeAgostini/Getty Images, p. 17; Ann Ronan Pictures/Print Collector/Getty Images, p. 18; Hanis/Getty Images, p. 20; Werner Forman/Universal Images Group/Getty Images, p. 21; alexander ruiz/Getty Images, p. 24; Hanan Isachar/Alamy Stock Photo, p. 25; Science History Images/Alamy Stock Photo, p. 27; Matt Hahnewald Photography/Alamy Stock Photo, p. 28; Paldas Photography/Getty Images, p. 30; Getty Images, p. 31; Fine Art Images/Heritage Images/Getty Images, p. 33; Science History Images/Alamy Stock Photo, p. 35; WHO image courtesy of NLM/NIH, p. 36; Edward S Curtis/Library of Congress, p. 40; gmc3101/Getty Images, p. 41; CM Dixon/Print Collector/Getty Images, p. 42; Wellcome Collection, p. 44; DEA/G. DAGLI ORTI/De Agostini/Getty Images, p. 47; Stock Montage/Getty Images, p. 48; Bibliothèque Interuniversitaire de Santé/Wikimedia Commons PD, p. 52; DEA/A. DAGLI ORTI/De Agostini/Getty Images, p. 53; PHAS/Universal Images Group/Getty Images, p. 57; DEA/G. NIMATALLAH/De Agostini/Getty Images, p. 60; DEA/A. DE GREGORIO/Getty Images, p. 63; Stefano Bianchetti/Corbis/Getty Images, p. 66; Wellcome Collection, p. 68. Design elements: AnK_studio/Shutterstock; Ezhevika/Shutterstock.

Cover image: Hulton Archive/Getty Images.